T0087906

The New Novello Choral Edition

NOVELLO HANDEL EDITION

General Editor Donald Burrows

Utrecht Jubilate

For 2 alto and bass soli, SATB chorus and orchestra

Edited by Watkins Shaw

Vocal Score

Novello London

Order No: 070148

CONTENTS

PREFACE

This work (HWV 279) was first performed at the thanksgiving for the Treaty of Utrecht held in St Paul's Cathedral, London, on 7 July 1713. Handel had its companion Te Deum (HWV 278) ready by the preceding January, but no precise date is known for the composition of this Jubilate setting. At the end of his autograph MS score he has written 'S D G / G. F. Hendel', underneath which we may be sure he would have entered the date in accordance with his usual practice. Unfortunately the leaf has been cropped in binding so that nothing now is legible below his signature other than the upper half of the figures '1713', the day and month having been quite cut away. Although the treaty was not signed until 31 March and was only made public in London during May, things were clearly in the wind. There is a newspaper report of a public rehearsal of Handel's Te Deum on 19 March in the Banqueting House, Whitehall. This might perhaps be taken as a loose journalistic use covering both Te Deum *and* Jubilate: the eventual performance in St Paul's was similarly referred to as of a Te Deum. According to Handel's endorsements on his MS score, the soloists on 7 July were:

No. 3, 'Be ye sure': 'Mr Hughs' (Francis Hughes), alto; 'Mr Wahle' (Samuel Weely), bass.

No. 5, 'For the Lord is gracious': 'Mr Hughs', alto I; 'Mr Elford' (Richard Elford), alto II; 'Mr Gates' (Bernard Gates), bass.

All were members of the Chapel Royal choir, though Weely did not receive an appointment to an established 'place' until Elford's death in 1714. Although Handel wrote Elford's part on a stave above that of Hughes, its compass is in fact the lower of the two, for which reason *these staves have been interchanged in the present edition*.

Together with the related Te Deum it quickly established itself in standard use on such occasions as the Festivals of the Sons of the Clergy, and became the kernel of the early Music Meetings of the three choirs of Gloucester, Hereford and Worcester. When, from 1743, that Te Deum tended to be overtaken in popularity by Handel's 'Dettingen' setting (HWV 283), this Jubilate of 30 years earlier continued in use with the later Te Deum which had no companion Jubilate of its own.

Along with HWV 278 it was published in score by Walsh, c.1731, described not as in celebration of the Treaty of Utrecht but as 'Perform'd before the Sons of the Clergy'. Earlier, during 1717-18 while he was associated with James Brydges (soon to become Duke of Chandos) at Cannons, Handel had recourse to the work and reduced its texture to a 3-part chorus (STB) and soprano, tenor, and bass soloists, also paring the instrumentation, to form the 'Chandos' Jubilate (HWV 246), generally known as 'Chandos Anthem No. 1'.

SOURCES

A British Library, RM 20.g.5. Handel's holograph MS written in the act of composition. Originally a separate fascicle, this is now bound with the related Te Deum score under the same 'call number', together with the addition of a single leaf carrying an alternative form of the ending to No. 3, 'Be ye sure'. The leaves containing the last 23 bars of No. 2, 'Serve the Lord', are now missing, and are known to have been wanting at the date of binding, sometime between c.1780 and 1800.

This is the prime source on which the present edition (other than the missing 23 bars) is exclusively based. There are numerous transcripts of a secondary nature, none of which modifies, amplifies, or elucidates the autograph in any material particular. But for the ending of No. 2 recourse has been had to **B** below, as appearing to have a close relationship to **A**, confirmed by **C**.

B British Library, Add. MS 5323. Score, in the hand of 'RM1' in J. P. Larsen's classification (though by some slip stated by Larsen himself to be in that of J. C. Smith).

C British Library, Egerton MS 2914. Score, in the hand of J. C. Smith the elder.

The following further MS transcripts (in score except where otherwise noted) have been consulted.

D Bentley, Hants. Collection of the late Gerald Coke.

E British Library, RM 18.f.9; **F** RM 19.a.14 (organ score); **G** Harleian MS 7342 (dated 1720).

H Cambridge, Fitzwilliam Museum, Music MS 814.

J Cambridge, University Library, Ely Cathedral MSS 12 and 14.

K Egham, Surrey. Bass part belonging to Dr Geoffrey Chew. This furnishes the vocal bass together with the instrumental bass in score, a curious form for which there seems no ready explanation.

L London, Royal College of Music, MS 888.

M Manchester Central Library, MS 130 Hd4 v.172.

N York Minster Library, MS M96.

X The Earl of Malmesbury possesses a MS score which belonged to Handel's friend Elizabeth Legh in 1718. Lord Malmesbury discouraged my request to examine it, feeling that his primary duty was to its preservation. But Donald Burrows kindly informs me that (a) it does not contain the curious revised ending to No. 3, and (b) the voice parts of No. 6 take the original form of bars 30-34, so conforming to other secondary sources in these two particulars.

Separate reference must be made to a further MS in the British Library, Add. MS 27745 (also including HWV 283, and therefore later than 1743), in view of a pencil note found on f.3 stating that it 'is the Organ Copy from which Handel played this composition at his Oratorios'. It is nothing of the kind, but amounts to a short score of the instrumental parts set out on two staves by an unidentified scribe in such a way as to be playable (though now and again a little awkwardly, as when it seeks to include sustained wind parts against moving strings) on a keyboard.

EDITORIAL PROCEDURE

Numbering of movements is editorial. C clefs for soprano, alto, and tenor voices are transcribed in the G clef, and the time signature $\mathbf{C}$ is rendered as $\frac{4}{4}$. Any material in square brackets is editorial, as is the italic text of No.4, which is offered as an alternative to allow singers greater opportunity to breathe. Many obviously missing ties have been silently supplied, and also cancelling accidentals in the modern convention. Handel's spasmodic figuring of the basso continuo is omitted as not indicating anything not disclosed by the obbligato parts.

KEYBOARD PART

As this is a work which choirs may very well wish to perform in church with organ accompaniment only (possibly with the addition of a pair of trumpets), Handel's instrumental score has been arranged for organ. His texture, however, is such that any form of keyboard arrangement must necessarily be free, and for this reason in Nos. 3 and 5 the true violin and oboe parts are shown for information on 'pearl' staves up to the points at which the keyboard reduction may serve without further clarification. In movements which include trumpets, these parts are, of course, subsumed in the general harmonic texture for the organ; but, where salient, these again are shown for information on a 'pearl' stave. If a performance with organ *and* trumpets is possible, it will be useful for the organist to know what the trumpet parts are. Small-size notes in the editorially-arranged keyboard part represent the filling of the basso continuo.

This organ arrangement has been so contrived that at rehearsals with piano it will be found adaptable and sufficient if any left hand notes other than the bass which are unplayable on the piano are omitted.

For purposes of performance with orchestra an independent editorial organ continuo part is available on hire.

ACKNOWLEDGEMENTS

I am grateful to Donald Burrows for discussion of certain matters, especially the problem of the alternative ending to No. 3.

WATKINS SHAW, January 1991

Textual Notes

As already stated, the text below is strictly based on **A**, slightly supplemented by **B** and **C**.

INSTRUMENTATION

Throughout his works generally, Handel was by no means explicit, let alone systematic or consistent, in naming his instrumental staves. Nevertheless, his intentions are often implicit enough to give little trouble, as, for example, when he writes 'tutti' against a G clef stave, which in certain contexts is clearly to be understood as indicating oboes doubling violins. But some discussion is necessary here in relation to oboes and bassoons.

His specific directions on his autograph MS, supplemented here in italic by clear implications, are as follows:

No. 1 Trumpets 1 and 2; *Violin 1/Oboe 1* sharing a stave; *Violin 2/Oboe 2* sharing a stave; *Viola.*
No. 3 Violin solo; Oboe solo. At bar 34, above top stave, 'tutti e forte' (*Violin 1/Oboe 1, Violin 2/Oboe 2; Viola*).

No. 5 Violins tutti; Oboes tutti. At bar 30, above top stave, 'tutti' (*Violin 1/Oboe 1, Violin 2/Oboe 2, Viola*).
No. 6 Trumpets 1 and 2; Oboes 1 and 2; Cello and Bassoon sharing a stave; Violins 1 and 2; Viola; Organ and Double Bass sharing a stave.

As to the instrumental bass generally, it will be seen that only in No. 6 does he specify the instruments required. Elsewhere organ, cello, and double bass may be taken for granted. But it cannot be supposed that, except in No. 6, bassoons are to be silent, and therefore an editorial part has been extracted for them from the general bass in all other movements on the lines employed by copyists contemporary with Handel when drawing out such instrumental parts, that is to say using them in full chorus work and in the instrumental ritornelli passages in solo movements, but silencing them in the accompaniment to solo passages.

The question of oboes arises with regard to Nos. 2, 4, and 7. One can hardly doubt that they would play in No. 2, and the reason they are not specified is clearly because, in the autograph score, this movement continues without a break on the same page as the ending on No. 1, separated only by a double bar, so that the intentions of No. 1 presumably continue in force, i.e., Oboes 1 and 2 doubling Violins 1 and 2. But a slight complication ensues in that, when instruments enter for the first time in this movement (bar 12), what are plainly – even though unlabelled – the violins are divided into Violins 1, 2, and 3. Of these, Violins 1 and 2 proceed to double each other until bar 35, suggesting, perhaps, that further doubling by Oboes 1 and 2 might be over-emphatic. Nevertheless, I suspect the copyist of Handel's orchestral parts would not be sensitive to this and would simply do the conventional thing, making Oboes 1 and 2 double Violins 1 and 2. So I have included such doubling in the oboe parts to this edition, leaving it to conductors to decide for themselves whether, in circumstances of present-day performance, to omit oboes in this movement.

No. 4 is in an 'antique' style of ecclesiastical vocal counterpoint with free instrumental parts. I have provided editorial oboe parts doubling soprano and alto voices, but there is probably something to be said for a relief from oboe tone in this movement.

One cannot conceivably suppose that oboes were not used in No. 7, forming the climax of the work, and I have assumed that Handel's copyists would have made them double Violins 1 and 2.

No. 1 'O BE JOYFUL'

Without explicit designation at the outset, Handel makes clear that the 3rd and 4th staves of his score are for Violin 1/Oboe 1 and Violin 2/Oboe 2 respectively by his instruction 'viol' [i.e., senza oboi] in bar 3, and 'tutti' [i.e., con oboi] in bar 4. See also bars 6, 7, 18, 35, and 38. But these directions are not comprehensive: 'tutti' is obviously called for in bar 29, 'viol' in bar 32, and the explicit 'viol' in bar 38 should have been followed somewhere (presumably in bar 39) by 'tutti', and so these have been supplied editorially. Bars 43-4 contain the characteristic 'viol' phrase, which therefore has also been marked thus editorially ('tutti' in consequence being similarly reintroduced at the end of bar 44) – but not without slight hesitation lest in this generally climactic choral passage violins with oboes might possibly have been intended throughout. Such a consideration could not, however, apply to bars 32-4 (despite the added sonority of the sustained trumpets and chorus at this point), unless, to avoid the low C sharp not available to early 18th-century oboes, Oboe 2 were adjusted by a copyist in some such way as

As to precisely how the oboes should bring to an end their phrases in bar 3 and corresponding places, it is opportune to recall that in the opening of *Laudate, pueri, dominum* (available in the Novello Handel Edition), the composer had earlier used what is in all relevant essentials the material of bars 2-4 of this Jubilate, marked in the same manner for violins and oboes. The oboe parts used under his direction at the first performance of *Laudate* still exist (Pierpont Morgan Library, New York, Koch Foundation Deposit 1085) and show that the copyist used his discretion by making the oboes end the phrase at what corresponds to the 3rd beat of bar 3 of the present work with a full crotchet $f\#^2$ and d^2 respectively. In the full score on hire connected with this edition, this (or corresponding) treatment has been adopted editorially in bars 3, 18, 32, and 43.

No. 3 'BE YE SURE'

Bar 33. At some date unknown after initial completion of the movement, Handel fashioned a different ending as shown in our Appendix. Perhaps this was in connection with some revival of the work. His autograph MS of it, on a single sheet of paper, is now bound at the end of his score, RM 20.g.5. His characteristic cue-marks in the shape of pencil 'flags' (now becoming faint) on the original form show where the substitution is to occur. Ordinarily one would give weight to a composer's revision as no doubt representing his more considered view, and would probably adopt it as the authoritative text. But here there are grounds for hesitation. Viewed subjectively, there seems no gain in effectiveness, unless it was specifically desired to eliminate a concluding ritornello. As for craftsmanship, when writing on a separate piece of paper Handel has overlooked the consecutive octaves arising between the alto and bass voices at the last notes of bar 32 and the first of his revised bar 33, or the uncomfortably 'near' octaves between violin and instrumental bass. No secondary source transmits this revision. Though suggestive, that in itself is not conclusive, for they may all have shared a common descent from a state anterior to this revision. But all in all, and especially in view of the unsatisfactory join following bar 32, it does not seem that this alternative commends itself for performance.

Bar 34 (original version). Here, where a stave obviously for violas is introduced, Handel contented himself merely with 'tutti e forte' over the highest stave of his score (hitherto for solo violin). But this cannot mean that the stave below continues to be, as hitherto, for solo oboe. Clearly at this point a 4-part ritornello is meant, the term 'tutti' meaning Oboes 1 and 2 doubling Violins 1 and 2.

No. 4 'O GO YOUR WAY'

Handel's bars in this movement, under the signature ₵, are sometimes of two, sometimes of four minims, though bars of two minims are the more prevalent. Bars of four minims have been preferred editorially.

Bars 51-3 and 66-8. In such passages a present-day publisher's reader might well ask a composer for clarification of his intended inflection of the note E on its several occurences. At first, until one is pulled up by the explicit flat in bar 53, one has no difficulty in accepting naturals in 51 and 52, but doubt then retrospectively arises, colouring bar 67 also. From time to time, especially in early works, Handel, having made a modulation, would be casual and inconsistent in inserting accidentals necessary thereafter, as though he were carrying a new key-signature in his head. This is not exactly parallel to the present case, but may shed light on his mental process here if thinking more in B flat than in F. With regard to bars 52-3, an earlier Novello editor, W. T. Best, resolved the matter by treating the flat in the soprano as a mistake, but this, though valid musically, seems not to hold water in the light of bar 68. However, he supplied flats to violin, voice, and instrumental bass of the last crotchet in bar 67, as did Samuel Arnold (*The Works of G. F. Handel*, 1789-97); but the rising violin phrase gives one a little hesitation, and it is a shade difficult to suppose that Handel omitted all three by mistake. Much depends on how far one *either* regards bars 52 and 67 as casually notated and bars 76-7 as at last revealing the true intent, *or* regards bars 52 and 67 as deliberately different from bars 76-7 with their markedly charged plagal preparation. Taking the latter view one might be content to leave Handel's notation as it is, though perhaps supplying a flat in the alto (not tenor) of bar 52. It does not seem to me that the matter is capable of convincing resolution, and the flats I have editorially supplied simply represent what I feel to be the balance of considerations.

No. 5 'FOR THE LORD IS GRACIOUS'

Bars 27-8. The texture of this passage, arrived at only after amendment to the violin part in the act of composition, betrays something less than the hand of a master. At first Handel seems to have intended the first two beats of the violin part of bar 28 to follow the Alto II voice. But, having gone no further, he changed this to achieve the dissonance of *e'* on the first beat against the voice part, not noticing the consecutive 5ths thus created across the barline with the (presumably already written) oboe part. That Handel particularly desired this *e'* is shown by his preservation of it in the re-cast 'Chandos' version (though with a different approach, involving a grammatical error of its own, and in a texture not applicable here). The consecutive 5ths could be eliminated by substituting *g'* for the first note in bar 28 of either violin or oboe; but by changing the violin part one sacrifices the *e'* to which Handel seems to have attached importance, and in the oboe part it is preferable to allow the preceding *a'* to rise. On the whole, therefore, though the consecutives are uncomfortably patent to the ear, perhaps it is best to leave the passage undisturbed.

Bar 31. Here, where Handel wrote 'tutti' over the highest stave, the state of things is analogous to that discussed under No. 3, bar 34 above, i.e., top stave: Violin 1 with Oboe 1; 2nd stave: Violin 2 with Oboe 2; and a 3rd stave now introduced for Viola.

No. 6 'GLORY BE TO THE FATHER'

Bars 17-18. On a superficial reading Handel's autograph appears to contain but one dynamic in these bars, *pp* to the 6th quaver of Bar 17. But between the 4th and 5th quavers of the present bar 17 he originally had 8 quavers marked *p*. When he cancelled these the *p* mark was lost and he did not notice that the surviving *pp* mark was now unsuitably early in the resulting shortened phrase. This is now editorially adjusted in accordance with bars 25-6.

Bars 28-9, Tenor II. One may explain the state of Handel's autograph by the following diagram (not a facsimile):

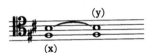

The note here marked (y), semibreve *b*, is firmly erased. The note here marked (x), semibreve *f♯*, superficially appears to have been erased, so that the bar has been taken to read *b – f♯*. But it seems possible that what may have happened is simply that the ink of the lower part of the note was slightly smeared before drying. It is very doubtful, in a context in which all other seven voices sustain a chord for a pair of tied semibreves, that a solitary part would during that time move from one harmony note to another, nothing being gained thereby. Moreover, to have Tenor II on *b* is unnecessary in the view of Basses I and II. There is no doubt that Handel intended the note (y) to be deleted; I suggest that in his mind the preceding *b*, to which it had been tied, was also cancelled. A comparison with bars 12-14 is not irrelevant. Be this as it may, I take responsibility for amendment to two tied semibreves, *f♯*.

Bar 29, Organ and Double Bass. Walsh's published score and all secondary MS sources except **K** have a semibreve *B* tied from bar 28, Handel's autograph has the reading

(i.e., running with cello and bassoon at the last three quavers), so conforming to bars 13 and 21. It is not impossible, however, that the first note was originally a semibreve, later altered to a minim when the subsequent quavers were squeezed into the bar. There is no doubt that the latter is the correct text.

Bars 30-34. The small notes and italic words of this edition show Handel's first form of these bars. One cannot say at what stage he chose to amend the articulation to the form shown in standard-size notation except to remark that he had arrived at that by the time he made his 'Chandos' adaptation. The original note values of the supporting harmonies of the trumpets, oboes, bassoons, cellos, double basses, and organ coincided with the original voice parts, likewise those of the violas in bars 33-4. Though neglecting the organ/double bass stave, Handel amended all the rest by simply putting a stroke through the tail of the first minim of each bar, and deleting the following minims and crotchets. Then he added a tie in the voice parts between bars 30 and 31, and made clear the new underlay of the words by writing this firmly beneath the lower bass voice.

Putting aside **X**, as to which I cannot speak, **N** (according to my reliable informant) stands alone among the secondary sources in giving the revised form consistently. All others which are relevant to the complete voice parts give them in the original form, with two curious features: (1) the supporting wind and bass instruments have the note values of the revised form; (2) the vocal basses (which Handel wrote on one stave) take the revised form (except in **J** and, in a rather muddled way, **G**). Source **B**, however, goes so far as to make some attempt, though not comprehensive, to amend the notation of the voice parts in the direction of Handel's revision. All this raises questions about transmission of text which, though of interest in themselves, are purely abstract, and do not affect the purpose of this edition to present an authoritative text. *The original version is shown here largely as a matter of information in view of its 18th-century currency, but without any recommendation that it should be performed.*

No. 7 'AS IT WAS IN THE BEGINNING'

Bars 20-63. The slurs to paired quavers in voice and string parts are not found in A except in the violin parts of bar 25. They are adopted from C, which in all likelihood is transmitting good contemporary authority for phrasing the pairs.

Bar 89, Trumpet 2. The result of Handel's heavy amendment to this bar is that it contains two crotchets only, d^2, a^1; it is left to our presumption that these can only fall on the 2nd and 3rd beats. Secondary sources inexplicably have the fuller

Whatever Handel's original may have been before amendment, it was clearly not that.

Solo and Chorus   O BE JOYFUL

* See important note on keyboard part, p.v

* sic

3

4

5

No. 2   Chorus   SERVE THE LORD WITH GLADNESS

7

SOPRANO I

10

12

No. 3   Duet BE YE SURE THAT THE LORD HE IS GOD

14

No. 4   Chorus   O GO YOUR WAY INTO HIS GATES

18

25   Man.   Ped.

29

20

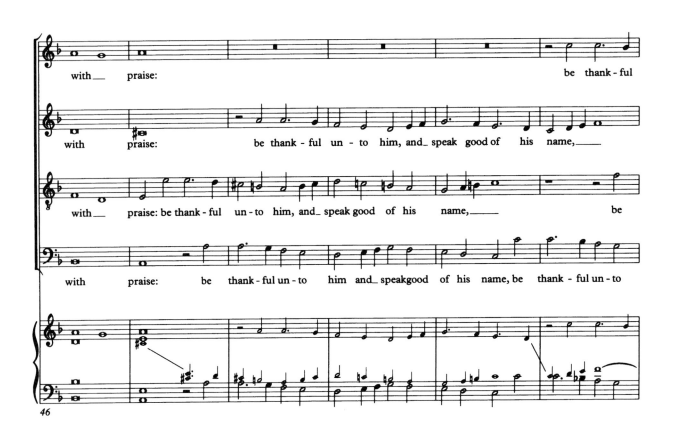

21

* See Preface, p.vi

Trio FOR THE LORD IS GRACIOUS

ALTO I: For the Lord is gra-cious, is gra-cious, is gra-cious, is gra-cious, his

ALTO II: -ing, for___ the Lord is gra-cious, is gra-cious, is gra-cious, is gra-cious,

BASS

ALTO I: mer - cy is ev-er-last-ing, is ev-er-last - - -

ALTO II: his mer-cy is ev-er-last - - - ing, his mer-cy is ev-er-

26

28

No. 6   Chorus GLORY BE TO THE FATHER

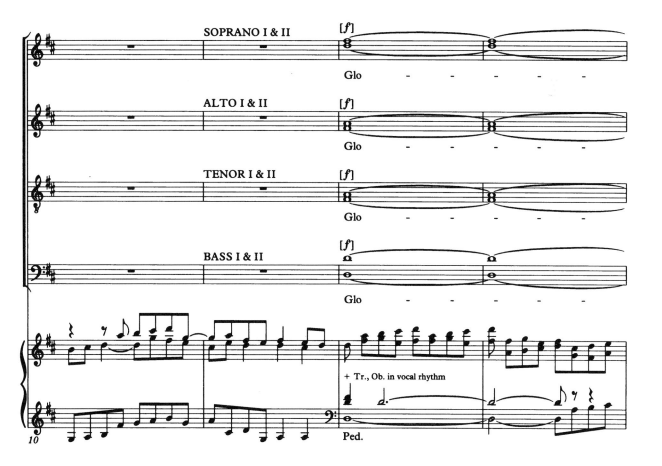

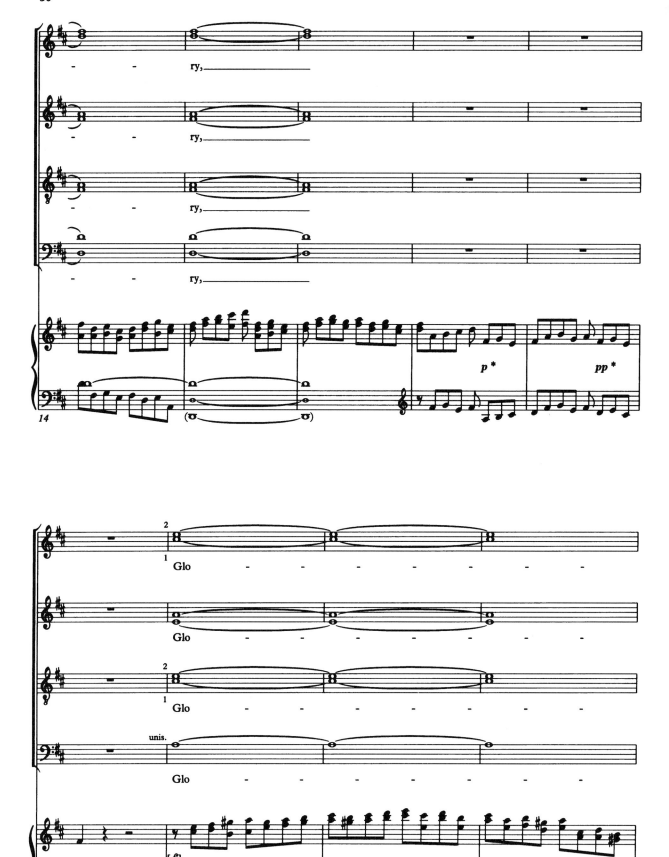

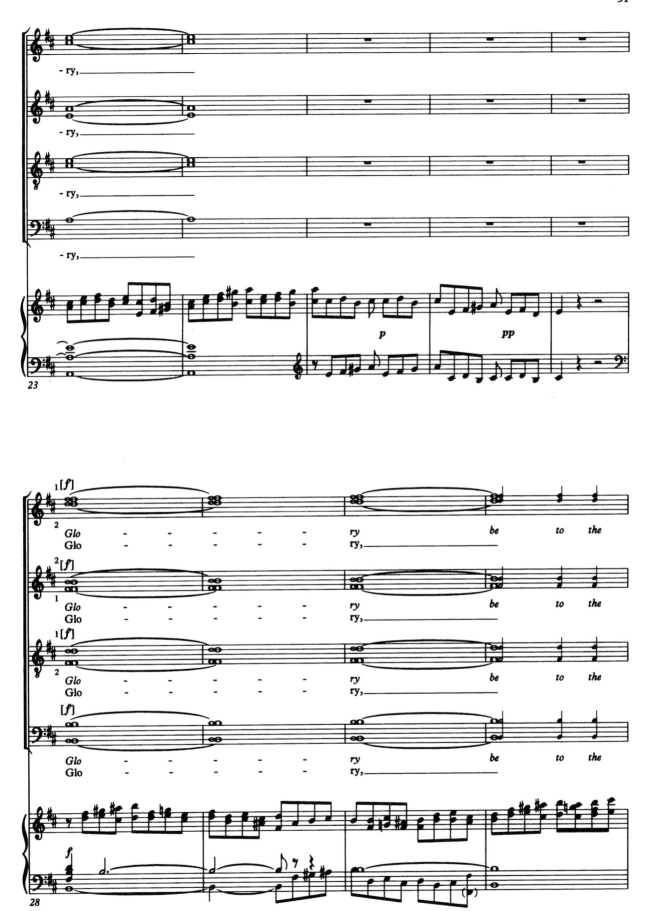

Bars 28-34. Small notes and italic text represent Handel's first version.

32

Son, and to the

Son, and to the

Son, and to the

Son, and to the

40

Ho - - ly Ghost;

Ho - ly Ghost;

Ho - ly Ghost;

Ho - ly Ghost;

p

[*pp*]

44

No. 7   Chorus AS IT WAS IN THE BEGINNING

36

* See Preface, p.viii

38

40

42

APPENDIX

Alternative ending to No. 3
(showing the join with bar 32 of page 15)